I went for a walk. I passed a wall and saw something move.
What could it be?

Ladybirds.

I passed a wood fence and saw something move.
What could it be?

Snails.

I passed some wild roses and saw something move.
What could it be?

Caterpillars.

I passed a pile of logs and saw something move.
What could it be?

Ants.

I passed some purple thistles and saw
something move.
What could it be?

A bee.

I passed some tall grass and saw something move.
What could it be?

A spider.

I passed a field of poppies and saw
something move.
What could it be?

Butterflies.

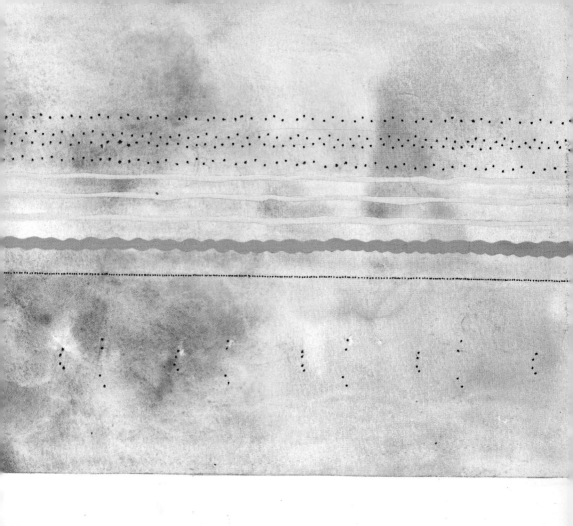

Now what could these be?

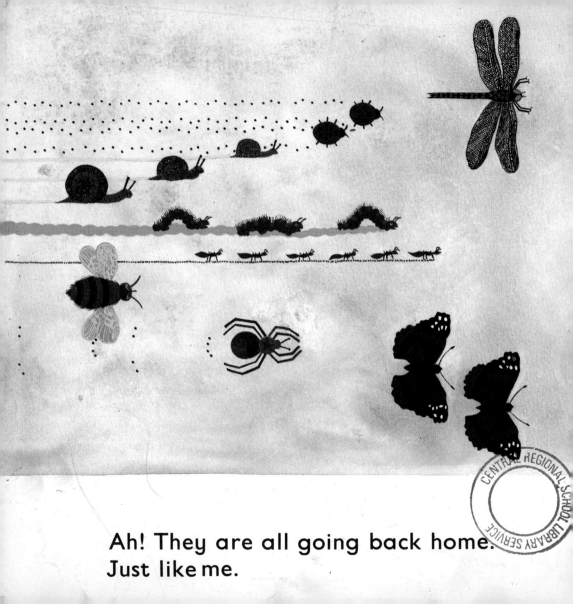

Ah! They are all going back home.
Just like me.